Haiku Workbook

Maryam Daftari

Haiku Workbook

Maryam Daftari

Copyright © 2022 Maryam Daftari

Published by 1st World Publishing
P.O. Box 2211, Fairfield, Iowa 52556
tel: 641-209-5000 • fax: 866-440-5234
web: www.1stworldpublishing.com

First Edition
Library of Congress cataloging-in-Publication Data
ISBN: 978-1-4218-3526-6

All rights reserved. No part of this book may be reproduced or utilized in any form or by any means, electronic or mechanical, including photocopying or recording, or by any information storage and retrieval system, without permission in writing from the author.

Dedication

For my grandson, Sam

and

for Cora and Myrna

Introduction

Contents

Preface 6

Introduction 8

Selected Haiku 20

Haiku and Pictures 26

References 140

Preface
Toward the Joy in Nature

Haiku shows it all —whether to child or adult — not only the beautiful, but the profound intricacies and realities of life in Nature.

What is more marvelous than to acquaint the child in each one of us — to be conscious of the joys in Nature, and to be able — in a special fun sort of way — to participate by describing what we observe! Moments of beauty captured in verse — like a shot of the camera!

Haiku endows children in primary school (and beyond) a creative and intuitive urge to be able to describe that monarch butterfly alighting on a bright pink zinnia, a dragonfly resting on the lake's lotus at a botanic garden, or the green turquoise hummingbird slurping nectar from a flaming orange trumpet vine. It fine tunes perceptive powers and the enthusiastic search for spotting and catching Nature's innumerable displays of beauty. From a young age, a child will want to preserve Nature's beauty.

****

Ever since I was introduced to haiku over a decade ago — or maybe the haiku was magically introduced to me, it has been a kind of love affair — gifting me a

Preface

special kind of inner joy. I wish I had made its acquaintance as a kid — many decades ago. This is why I am presenting this little haiku workbook for children and those who are interested and curious about Nature's amazing ways.

****

When I lived in Fairfield, Iowa, my next door neighbors had twins: two lovely girls, Cora and Myrna. I saw them ever since they were born, pretty much every day or several times a week until they were four and a half years old. And we have been in touch ever since I came to San Diego. Now that they are older, it came to my mind to write a book of haiku for them to explore the joy of poetic expression. What a great time to familiarize them with poetry! I thought I would dedicate this book to them specifically, and to other children generally who may be interested in enjoying and creating haiku for its beauty, simplicity and fun . There is no better learning than doing --and so this evolved to become a haiku workbook: how to read and enjoy haiku, how to observe the intriging world of Nature, or even to look at nature pictures, and try to write your own haiku. Easy, fun, and meaningful!

HAIKU WORKBOOK

Introduction

Poetry has many styles and forms. One of them is the haiku.
This is a workbook on haiku, and is meant to be used to practically learn how to write short poems called haiku.

A poem succeeds when its story comes alive, and you are there vicariously with the poet, seeing, feeling what the poet describes. A poem truly succeeds when the reader remembers the poem, leaving an indelible impression on his/her mind.

If you were sitting in a movie theater watching a movie, then reading a poem like the haiku, could be like jumping, splashing into the screen and becoming part of the movie.

A poet is an observant person who experiences something and is able to express his/her feelings with the music of words so that others can also feel what the poet felt, often reaching into some principle, some truth that transcends that unique experience. A poet captures thoughts and feelings of a moment or moments that can be a shared with others: happy / sad, pensive / hopeful, frustrated / relaxed.

Introduction

How to use this (work)book.

I hope you enjoy the haiku and photographs of Nature in this book. In case you want to try your hand at writing haiku, I have provided a couple of areas on some pages with blank lines so that you can use them to draft a version of your haiku, and then under the picture, your final version after you have revised your poem.

I encourage you to look at the picture, or at a specific scene in Nature or imagine one you have seen and experienced, using it as a motivation to write your own haiku.

Here are some suggestions for readers / writers, whether children, home-schooling parents or interested teachers.

A Note to Parents and Teachers

Parents can read the introduction and work with children to either think of a scene, feel inspired by Nature, or to look at the pictures, like the ones illustrated in order to describe the image and their feelings in the moment.

HAIKU WORKBOOK

A Note to Children

You can explore this workbook at your leisure, and try writing some haiku after first reading the **Introduction** to learn and get a feel for the fun of composing haiku. Look at the photo. What do you see? Can you write down what you observe in each photo -- as though you are on the phone and want to describe what you see to a friend.

Vivid poetry gifts you with joy, beauty, and stories of life. And the haiku you will be reading about and learning to write, mirror Nature and life. Haiku does this in a special way because it can change the way you see the world, especially the unbounded world of Nature. This is why this little workbook of haiku will acquaint you with short, vivid, and vibrant poetry in the form of images : that is the magic of haiku! It focuses on just a sliver of Nature's grandeur, a bird's eye view, while at the same time, placing it in a wider context by making you think of the meaning of the image you see as it relates to Nature and even your own life. Those three short lines whether written or read, communicate a unique captured instance of Nature's beauty -- like a photo or mirror. What you see, you express in your haiku — as is. You can be an excited "gazer" and writer of Nature's wonders! It is like magic but real!

Introduction

Watercolor Painting by Author

HAIKU WORKBOOK

The **haiku** originated in Japan, and typically has a total of 17 syllables. Each haiku is divided into three lines:

Line 1: 5 syllables : Lady in garden

Line 2: 7 syllables : flowers and trees talk to her

Line 3: 5 syllables : love affair takes off

Although varying interpretations of the form have evolved through the centuries, and some write their haiku without counting syllables (what has also been called sound units in English or "on" in Japanese), many poets prefer adhering to the rules.

Line 1: a shorter line

Line 2: a longer line

Line 3: a shorter line

The word **haiku** is derived from the Japanese word **hokku** meaning "starting verse." The *"hai"* of haiku can mean "joke or fun or unusual." Basically, haiku is a short poem about nature. The beauty of the haiku lies in its love for and closeness with Nature — describing Nature as you see it — at this *very moment* in time!

Introduction

What do you see out there? Be specific! What does it do to you? How does it make you feel? How does it make you think? What does it mean to you in this instant in time?

There creeps a certain kind of joy in your heart when you look at Nature! Describe it there and then! What does it remind you of? What do you witness — what is your feeling? In other words, haiku focuses on a brief "staccato" moment in time!

It is a way of looking at the physical world and seeing something deeper. Haiku uses simple words and keen observations to describe scenes in nature. One writer of haiku, Jane Reichhold, from whose book "Writing and Enjoying Haiku," I have used quite a few ideas in this introduction, talks about one theory that believes the haiku should not be any longer than one breath. However, she points out that to read a haiku, you will need two breaths!

 What is fun and exciting about writing haiku for anyone, especially for children, is that you can connect it with your daily life. We are not separate from Nature. Just look out the window! What do you see out the window, in a park or at a botanic garden? Use your five senses. It is such fun to create a haiku! A work of art in words.

For many, it may be both simple and difficult to write haiku because besides what you observe, you have to be able to describe the "thingness" – the essence or spirit of what is out there that you are trying to communicate to the reader.

As the writer, you want the reader to experience what you saw – something in the past – in that moment. But you must write it in the present tense! Haiku is not about what you think, but about what you experience. And to be able to share it in such a way so that the reader can experience it too. You are sharing your unique experience and permitting the reader to use her/his own visualization and imagination.

 Although it is better to avoid capital letters or punctuation, some poets use them anyway. One haiku poet's tip for writing haiku makes it even simpler when she advises:

"Write haiku in three short lines, using the principle of comparison, contrast, or association. In haiku," Betsy Drevniok says, "the some-

Introduction

thing and something else are set together in clearly stated images. Together they complete and fulfill each other as one particular event."

The idea is to point the reader to understand that the idea of comparison is to show how two different things can be similar or share similar aspects. Another technique is to contrast images. These are images expressed in words by the haiku.

You can also use the technique of association – how different things relate or come together as one. In other words, you may try to show how everything is part of everything else. That's Nature!

In the following pages, where I have a haiku on the left page and a picture on the right page, note that the picture on the right will probably depict only one of the images that the haiku mentions in words.

Ultimately, after reading many, many haiku -- old and new, you will settle on the "rules" you like most and are comfortable with. Many lovers of haiku have come to the conclusion that there is no one way of writing haiku. So within the framework of observing Nature in the now — this moment — write what you see and feel! See Nature in action at a certain moment – this very moment that you witness!

A haiku is usually divided into two sections. Preferably it should not be a run-on sentence or be a complete sentence with each line running clearly into the next.

In other words, a haiku needs a "syntactical break," separating it into two clearly visible divisions. The shorter part — which can be either the first short line or the last short line — is referred to as "the fragment," and the longer portion (or two-line remainder of the haiku) is called "the phrase." But then, some haiku writers may not exactly follow this. If this seems too complicated, forget about it.

You may come to think there are too many rules in composing a haiku. Relax. There are many people who write haiku and are not bound by all the so-called rules. Writing haiku means you want to enjoy Nature and write what you see. Observation and a brief description is the key!

It is wise not to forget that your haiku be written specifically in the present tense! What you see and experience in Nature at this very moment! What do your eyes see? You present "the thing" as is: you **show** — but you do not *tell* the reader what to think. If you are writing about something you experienced before, bring your mind to *that* moment,

Introduction

relive it in your memory. A reverence for Nature in what you write!

The "haiku attitude" is "nonjudgmental!" You view Nature as is and write what you see, preferably with a seasonal word or reference. In a haiku, the reader reads between the words you have written, between the lines. Brevity is important – it is key to good haiku writing. If you do not want to count syllables, just remember that the first line has to be short, the second line longer, the third, short again. If you are really attached to using "ing," (a gerund) -- use it! You are still in the present when you add "ing" to a verb. Many use the gerund form. Do not feel you are in a straightjacket! You are free to create!

Gaze outside any window in your house or apartment, in your backyard or park -- listen, observe – ***write your own haiku***. Haiku embraces simplicity and humility. Nature is beautiful but simple. Its majesty and grandeur gifts us a feeling of humility and connectedness with the world around us. Ultimately, the point of haiku is to enjoy Nature. If the rules bother you, let it not get in your way of writing. Write the way you like – as long as you write what you see ***in this moment*** in Nature – in the NOW! (Line 1: short, line 2: longer, line 3: short). Because we are writing in English and not Japanese, some "rules" have to be flexible. And haiku should be fun. It is fun! You may also write haiku from things inside your house – your pets, flowers, vegetables – whatever. You can create your own unique haiku.

From page 20, there are some beautiful Japanese haiku for you to enjoy, and then a few from other non-Japanese haiku poets. As you will see, there are varying interpretations concerning haiku writing. And as I have mentioned before, and would like to reemphasize, there is a great deal of freedom in crafting haiku despite the rules. You will discover the joy in creating your own unique haiku and sharing it. Open your eyes and your heart! Observe and be aware of your beautiful natural surroundings. Observing Nature carefully shows us to pause -- to look around us – to be present in the moment, whether in ordinary or unique moments, and to take pleasure in what we see. You may find you are now more aware of what you see in your daily life. Relax and be aware of this precious moment – relish in the moment of now! As you will see below, translating Japanese haiku into English is not easy, and may not follow the 5-7-5 rule.

sunset paints colors
dreams mix with flowers
& trees
stroll in paradise

Examples of Haiku from other Poets

In the next section (pages 20-25), I have selected some haiku from ancient and also contemporary poets to give you a feel for what haiku feels and sounds like. After that (page 26), you can read some of my own haiku written over the years, along with my camera shots that may serve as a visual description that is related to the verse. I hope you will enjoy this section as well.

old pond
a frog jumps in
the sound of water
(Matsuo Basho)

on a bare branch

a crow lands

autumn dusk

(Matsuo Basho)

the whole sky
in a wide field of flowers
one tulip
(Yosa Buson)

> a swinging gate
> on both sides flowers
> open – close
> (H. Takako)

amid fog

to clear cicada cries

dawn comes

(H. Takako)

> stuck in a vase
> deep mountain magnolia
> blossoms open
> (M. Shuoshi)

HAIKU WORKBOOK

summer river
there's a bridge but the horse
goes through water
(M. Shiki)

                        evening breeze
                    water laps the legs
                      of the blue heron
                        (Yosa Buson)

                                            across a rose fence
                                                a cat lover
                                                a cat hater
                                              (Kazuo Sato)

Introduction

first light
everything in this room
was already there
(Christopher Herold)

> **ever lingering**
> **in the taste of walnut**
> **deep autumn**
> **(James Hackett)**

> > **lily**
> > **out of the water**
> > **out of itself**
> > **(Nicholas Virgilio)**

                    winter morning
               without leaf or flower
                  shape of the tree
                  (L.A. Davidson)

the homeless man
takes off his shoes before
his cardboard house
(Penny Harter)

                        i catch
                    the maple leaf
                    then let it go
                    (John Wills)

Introduction

>deer licking
>first frost
>from each other's coats
>(Kobayashi Issa)

what a strange thing
to be alive
beneath cherry blossoms
(Kobayashi Issa)

>goes out,
>comes back –
>the loves of a cat
>(Kobayashi Issa)

tadpoles become frogs

caterpillars -- butterflies

what do you become?

_____

_____

_____

squirrels frolic on grass

weeping willow branches wait

swinging dance awaits

_____

_____

_____

Maryam Daftari

red roses swimming

in a mirror of a lake

memories reflect

_____

_____

_____

_____

_____

_____

summer dreams of fall

fall dreams of cold winter winds

seasons get mixed up

_____

_____

_____

sun's flushed face fading

reflected on sea's body

a departing kiss

hummingbird dances

trumpet flowers await guest

nature's miracles

_____

_____

_____

light as a feather

movement and rest balancer

green colors bewitch

_____

_____

_____

sea mirrors sun's face

azure red-gold flirt and mix

wet fiery kisses

_____

_____

_____

HAIKU WORKBOOK

setting sun/sea partner

nature's color orchestra

now -- bedtime stories

_____

_____

_____

ranunculous skirt

ballerina's red tutu

dance of the flowers

_____

_____

_____

Maryam Daftari

_____

_____

_____

sun's flushed face fades

reflecting on sea's body

a departing kiss

_____

_____

_____

HAIKU WORKBOOK

bamboo's arrow leaves

lotus awake on a lake

painter's dream come true!

_____

_____

_____

Maryam Daftari

_____

_____

_____

bird seesaws on branch

butterfly kisses jasmine

sky sees everything

_____

_____

_____

Maryam Daftari

queen-like lotus shines

mountain pouring waterfall

my art teacher's brush

_____

_____

_____

Maryam Daftari

_____

_____

_____

chinese painting glows

color dancing wild with brush

piece of nature cut

Painting by Author

HAIKU WORKBOOK

rosebuds unopened

busy bee always at work

spring is still asleep

_____

_____

_____

Maryam Daftari

hummingbirds long gone

naked branches dreaming green

greyness takes over

_____

_____

_____

plum blossoms raise heads

hummingbirds hover to kiss

beauty of rebirths

_____

_____

_____

flower greets each guest

both hummingbird/ bee happy

to each its own

_____

_____

_____

turtle drags its shell

oh, the rabbit's hurried hops

you arrive – sometime!

_____

_____

_____

rainbow colors reign

march to june ranunculus

magic of the sun

_____

_____

_____

Maryam Daftari

HAIKU WORKBOOK

we basque in beauty

every sunset different

memories crowding

_____

_____

_____

Maryam Daftari

humminbird hovers

on Mexican purple sage

dance of joyous feast

_____

_____

_____

lotus emerges

from dark waters — magical!

impeccably pure

_____

_____

_____

Maryam Daftari

fly, hover to feast

hummer flower encounter

survival comes first

_____

_____

_____

dreams floating in mind

moon takes over reigns of night

we hug/kiss goodnight

_____

_____

_____

our sheepadoodle

cross between Snoopy/Panda

I dream yin and yang

_____

_____

_____

gardenia's white skirt

ballerina's tulle tutu

rain's nourishing kiss

_____

_____

_____

Maryam Daftari

eyes in winter sleep

waking up with laughter sweet

ahh! snowing outside

_____

_____

_____

run and jump in glee

heart will join in jubilee

summer holidays

_____

_____

_____

Maryam Daftari

flowers rustling

hiding secrets in their hearts

nature knows secrets

_____

_____

_____

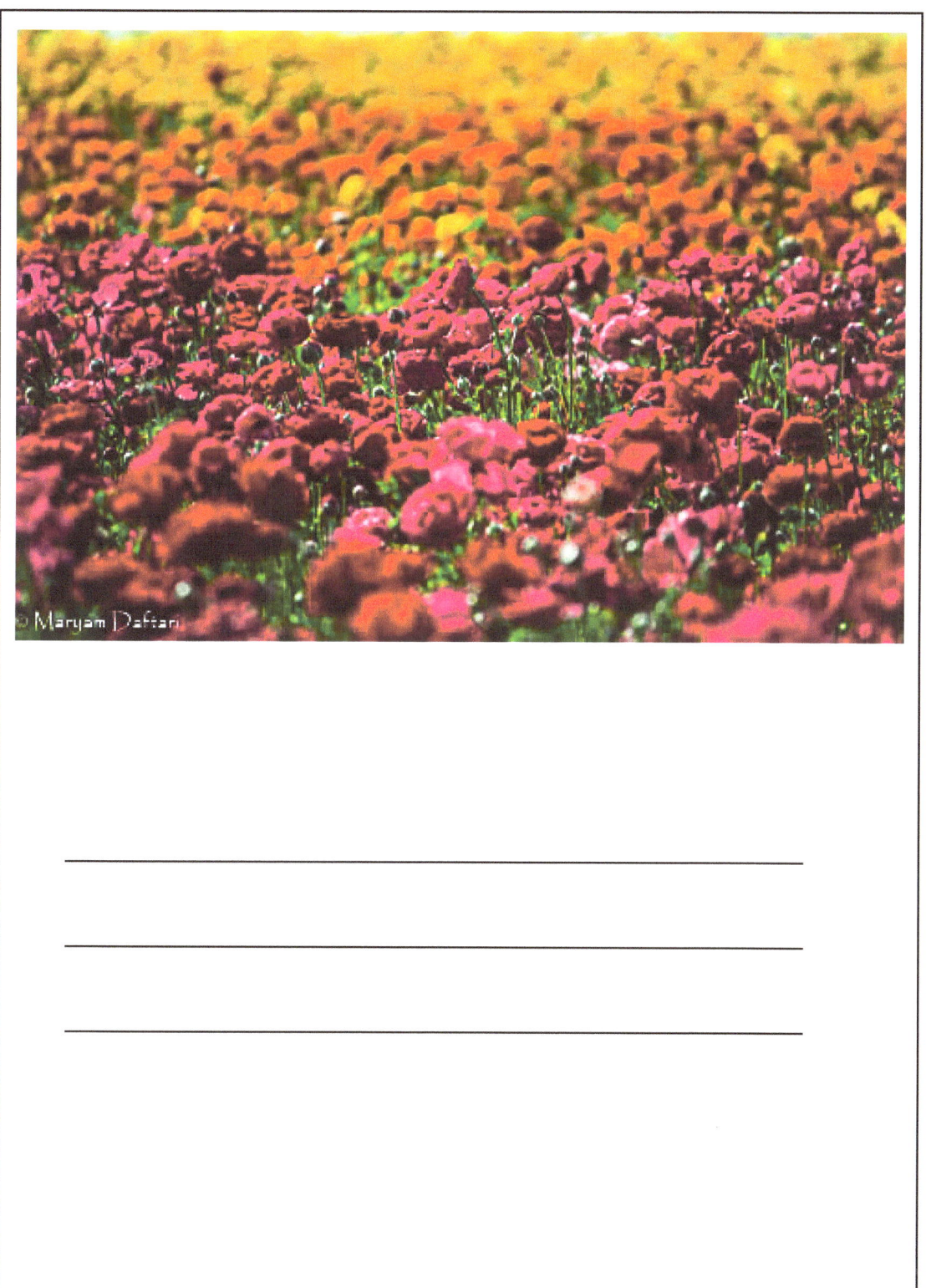

cherry blossoms sway

cover ground in white and pink

spring is speaking now

_____

_____

_____

spring is whispering

reflections bring memories

pray deeply for peace.

_____

_____

_____

hummingbirds are back

life is pulsating away

now to find nectar

_____

_____

_____

ice covers round pond

underneath -- leftover pods

lotus dreams rebirth

_____

_____

_____

HAIKU WORKBOOK

seeds now flowers

earth prepares for many births

we dream spring, summer

_____

_____

_____

Maryam Daftari

tuberose grows tall

eager to show white flowers

scent announces it

_____

_____

_____

raspy caws of crows

perched on our big walnut tree

nest of chicks — fly -- fall

leaves -- clues to seasons

autumn colors in full swing

joy is in your heart

_____

_____

_____

close your eyes and dream

dream lotus – waterlilies

summer's gifts flowing

_____

_____

_____

_____

_____

_____

dahlia after rain

flower resembles beehive

nature's patterns daze

_____

_____

_____

squirrel holding prize

with sharp teeth and his strong paws

winter's coming fast

_____

_____

_____

bamboo leaf droplets

tears flooding my eyes now

each moment, one drops

_____

_____

_____

zinnia's June guest

flutter of butterfly wings

eggs are left as gifts

_____

_____

_____

full moon of August

peeps into your warm window

dreams -- of hugging moon

_____

_____

_____

the sun of flowers

shimmering golden roses

beckon to you -- come!

_____

_____

_____

spring knocks every year

at the door of our hearts

whispers: "Time for love!"

_____

_____

_____

sapphire Tower blooms

blue-green flower spikes protect

nosy animals

_____

_____

_____

rose gifts its beauty

gently dives into your soul

a meditation

_____

_____

_____

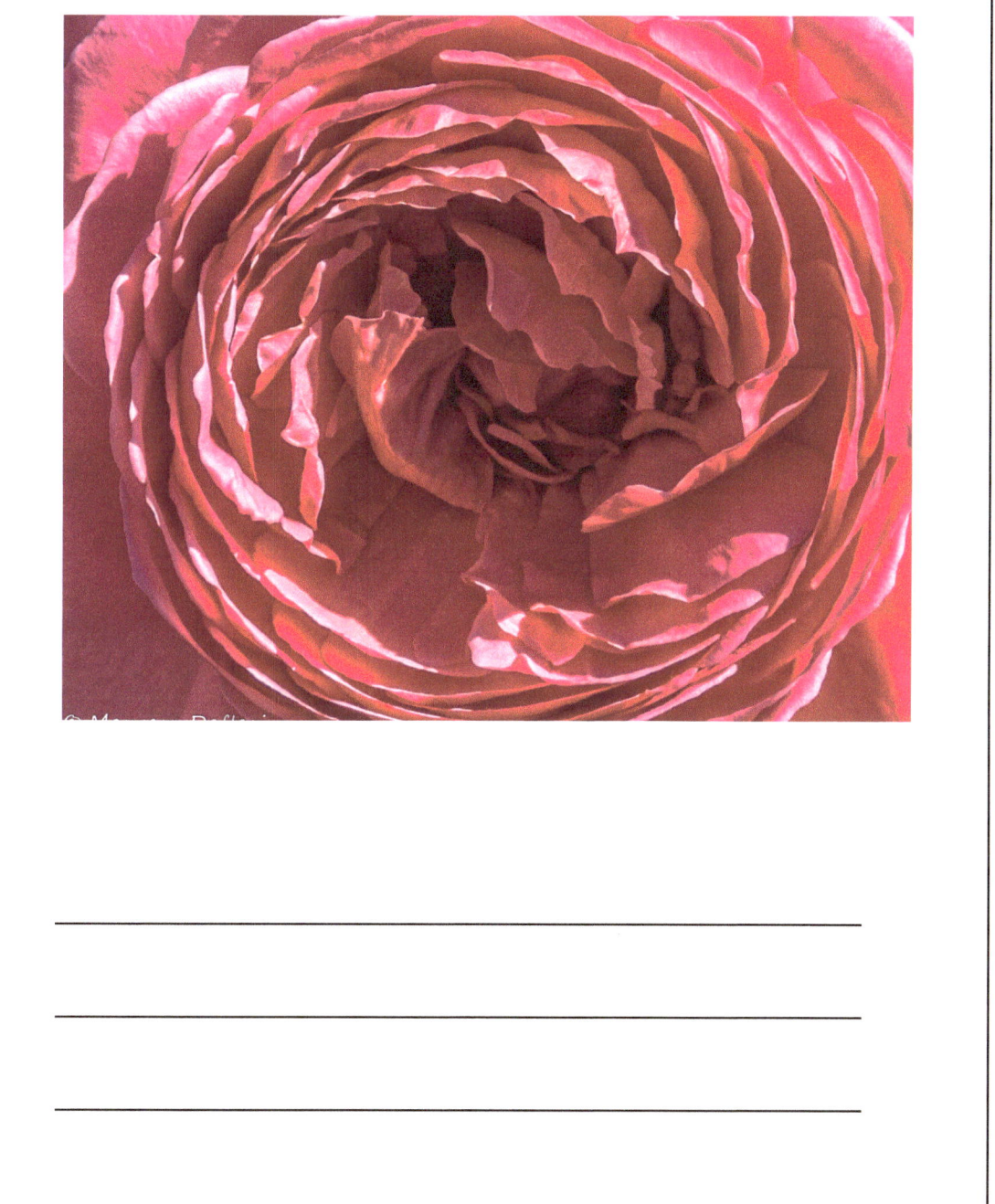

plumerias pose

as if nothing amiss

wish we could mimic

piling autumn leaves

scattered away by cold wind

rival colors fly

_____

_____

_____

Maryam Daftari

january rose

dancer's orange-layered skirt

scent of Mom's perfume

_____

_____

_____

[write your own haiku here]

_____

_____

_____

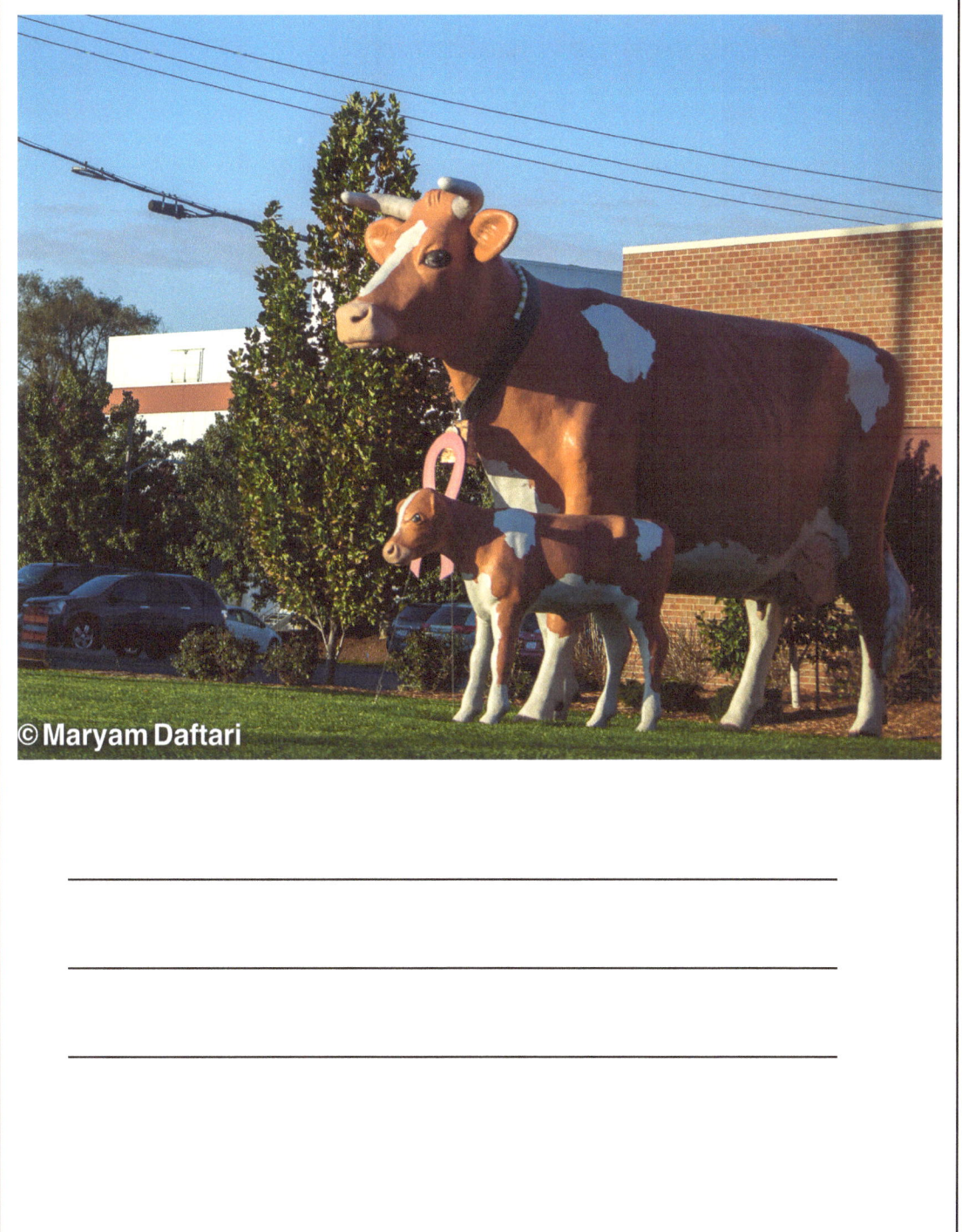

HAIKU WORKBOOK

[write your own haiku here]

_____

_____

_____

2017

HAIKU WORKBOOK

[write your own haiku here]

_____

_____

_____

HAIKU WORKBOOK

[write your own haiku here]

_____

_____

_____

HAIKU WORKBOOK

_____

_____

_____

References

[1] Yosa Buson, *Collected Haiku of Yosa Buson* (Copper Canyon Press, 2013)

[2] Matsuo Basho. *Basho: The Complete Haiku* (Kodansha, 2008)

[3] *The Essential Haiku: Versions of Basho, Buson, & Issa* (Turtleback Books, 1995)

[4] Nicholas Virgilio. *A Life in Haiku* (Turtle Light Press, 2018)

[5] Christopher Herold. *Inside Out: Haiku* (Red Moon Press, 2021).

[6] James Hackett. *The Way of Haiku: An Anthology of Haiku Poems. Poetry and Photos* (Japan Publications, 1969)

[7] L.A. Davidson, Laura Tanna. *My Fifty Favorite Haiku* (D L T Associates, Incorporated, 2017)

[8] Penny Harter, William J. Higginson. *The Haiku Handbook -25th Anniversary Edition: How to Write, Teach, and Appreciate Haiku* (Kodansha USA, 2013)

[9] Patricia Donegan , *Haiku Mind: 108 Poems to Cultivate Awareness and Open Your Heart* (Shambala, 2010)

[10] Robert Hass, *The Essential Haiku,* (The Ecco Press; 2012th edition (August 1, 1995))

[11] Jane Reichhold, *Writing and Enjoying Haiku* (Kodansha, USA, 2002)

References

www.ingramcontent.com/pod-product-compliance
Lightning Source LLC
Chambersburg PA
CBHW041535220426
43663CB00002B/43